The Church and the Churches

The Church and the Churches

Karl Barth

with a Foreword by
William G. Rusch

William B. Eerdmans Publishing Company
Grand Rapids, Michigan / Cambridge, U.K.

© 1936, 2005 Wm. B. Eerdmans Publishing Co.

First edition, 1936
This edition, 2005

Wm. B. Eerdmans Publishing Co.
255 Jefferson Ave. S.E., Grand Rapids, Michigan 49503 /
P.O. Box 163, Cambridge CB3 9PU U.K.

Printed in the United States of America

10 09 08 07 06 05   7 6 5 4 3 2 1

Library of Congress Cataloging-in-Publication Data

Barth, Karl, 1886–1968.
The church and the churches / Karl Barth. — New ed.
p.   cm.
ISBN-10: 0-8028-2970-8 (pbk.: alk. paper)
ISBN-13: 978-0-8028-2970-2
1. Church. 2. Sects. 3. Christian union.   I. Title.

BV600.3.B378   2005
280′.042 — dc22
2005050060

www.eerdmans.com

Contents

Foreword

S ome writings are deemed to be "classics" on the basis of their acknowledged excellence and enduring significance. These works, of course, represent only a small fraction of the countless efforts to put pen to paper or, in our day, words to computer screens. Although classics retain the limitations of time and space, they continue to speak with a freshness and relevance that at times can be startling.

The number of texts produced by the modern ecumenical movement that can claim the status of classic is relatively small. This is, no doubt, true because of both the short history of this movement and the nature of its texts. The two World Council of Churches statements on the unity of the church from the New Delhi and Canberra assemblies (1961, 1991) and the Faith and Order text *Baptism, Eucharist and Ministry* (1982) may perhaps be given this exalted status.

The succinct text from 1936 by Karl Barth presented in this volume, *The Church and the Churches,* is rarely listed among the classics of the ecumenical movement. It is easily overlooked in the plethora of documents that has emerged from the movement or in light of its author's monumental *Church Dogmatics.* Yet this communication, addressed by Barth to the global Second World Conference on Faith and Order which was held in Edinburgh, Scotland, in 1937, has every right to be considered one of the classic ecumenical texts of the twentieth century.

It is a faithful witness to its time and place:

its non-inclusive language may well be discordant to many a contemporary ear; its references to the religious and political situation in the Germany of its time perhaps no longer apply; the nearly seventy years that have passed since 1936 have seen changes in relationships between many churches. In sum, ecumenical reflection, experience, and action have made the world of the 21st century vastly different from that of the 1930s. Nevertheless, *The Church and the Churches* continues to speak freshly as an intense imperative transcending the intervening time. It can, moreover, be seen as addressing especially, although surely not only, churches in North America which now stand — in a new century and context — on the threshold of their own projected Second Conference on Faith and Order in North America. Barth's words remind us all of old lessons that should have been learned but now seem to have been forgotten.

Barth spoke in this concise text to the forthcoming Edinburgh Conference on Faith and Order of 1937. Now, through the renewed efforts of the original publisher, his message is again placed before churches that remain in disunity. The veracity and urgency of the message have not diminished. As Barth reminded his readers some seventy years ago, "'Homesickness for the *una sancta*' is genuine and legitimate only insofar as it is a disquietude at the fact that we have lost and forgotten Christ and with Him have lost the unity of the Church. . . . If we listen to the voice of the Good Shepherd, then the question of the unity of the Church will most surely become for us a burning question."

This challenge rings as true today as it did in yesteryear. Christians in broken churches and a fragmented world still need to hear the summons. Karl Barth once again speaks to another generation.

WILLIAM G. RUSCH
Festival of the Holy Trinity, 2004

The Church and the Churches

The Unity
of the Church

"The Church and the Churches" is the subject before us; it is obviously intended to suggest the question of the unity of the Church in view of the multiplicity of the churches. That question may be prompted by a variety of motives, which I need only indicate here.

We recall the fact that in hundreds of mission areas in Asia and Africa the Church is wrestling with the ancient religions, higher and lower, of the so-called heathen races. But where, who, and what is the Church? What a dissipation of the spiritual and material energies of the mission work arises from the fact that there is not one Church but many, and what a hindrance to the hearing of its message, what a bewilderment to its less attentive hearers, what a burden to the more serious, is the fact that these churches are in manifold conflict with each other.

We recall, moreover, that in its homelands,

evangelized for a millennium and more, the Church is today confronted with this and that religion of recent or brand-new formation — religions which surpass the old paganisms in power and light only because they make their appearance as religion under a disguise; under the disguise of moral, aesthetic, sanitary, social and political schemes for betterment, beneath which their religious *genii* remain concealed, save when their less cautious or their weaker-minded adherents draw the veil aside. The Church, which on this front ought to be waging a well-planned and active campaign, is not in a position to make it clear, against these adversaries, what it is, what it purposes, or in what precise way it differs from them. It is split up, as in Germany we have cause enough in recent years to know, into a multiplicity, into a number of divided and opposing camps; nor is it in this respect in better case than

6

are the profoundly divided "churches" of modern secularism. In such a shape as this the Church is wholly unable to make good its claim to possess a loftier message than theirs.

Further, none of us can fail to see that today as always it is the task of the Church to submit and subordinate itself on its human side, the side of its life, order, and teaching, to the standard which it derives from Christ, from God: its task is to exercise self-criticism, to purify itself from any element which is foreign to its origin and essence, and which, having such an essence and origin, it ought not to tolerate: it must look back to its origin and essence, set its compass by that bearing, suffer itself to be purged and reformed by that standard. But for such resolve the Church would need a unison of will and direction, without which every effort in these directions would only mean a continuance and intensification of the conflict between the several churches; and who can be sure that that conflict would really further the process of purging the reformation?

But let us lastly go on to consider what the Church is, what it ought to mean, for its own members, for those who are brought together within it through baptism, through the Word of God, through the Holy Communion; "the Church of the living God, the pillar and ground of the truth" (1 Tim. 3:15). Can it and will it be, as such, continually imposing, credible, convincing to its members, if as a Church it has its being only in an array of various churches, each of which represents to the others a problem, a critic, a rival, possibly also a disturber and an enemy? Concerned as we are with the true faith, is not the possibility, or rather the inevitability, of a comparison of faith with faith a menace to faith itself? What is the Church, if it can only present itself as repeating the manifoldness and contradictions of the world of pagan religions? Certainly, in that great process, so clearly discernible in the last two centuries, by which so many members have found themselves alienated from the Church, this actual multiplicity of the churches has been one of the strongest factors.

Such, more or less, are the motives which lead us now to set before us the question of church unity.

Yet it must be made clear at the outset that all these motives are merely secondary when compared with another authoritative impulse which forces this question upon us, and alone has the right to compel our attention to it. I refer to that one and only imperative and obligatory task from which the Church derives its existence, a task which lies upon every man who, as a responsible being has accepted the cause of the

Church as his own. This task emerges immediately from the fact that the one and only Word of God has once for all been uttered, for all men to heed, in the fact of the Incarnation: in the man Christ Jesus, in whom the sin of all men, their contradiction against God and their own inner self-contradiction is done to death, taken away, forgiven, and exists no more. The task from which the Church derives its being is to proclaim that this has really happened and to summon men to believe in its reality. It has therefore no life of its own, but lives as the body of which the crucified and risen Christ is the Head; that is to say, it lives in and with this commission. The same thing is true of each individual who is a member of this body. It is this task and commission which fundamentally impels and compels us to ask after the unity of the Church.

The task as thus committed contemplates no

multiplicity of churches. The New Testament speaks of a variety of communities, of gifts, and of persons within the one Church. But this manifoldness has no independent significance. Its origin, its rights, and its limits are to be found in the unity, or rather in the One, in Jesus Christ as the one Son of God, the bestower of the one Holy Spirit. Its basis does not lie (even of the good in God's creation the same thing must be said) in any independent rights and claims of local, national, cultural, or personal individuality. Like the unity of the Church, it has its basis in God's grace, and in no second principle distinguishable from grace. It is indeed, in itself, nothing else than the living unity of grace, the one body of Christ in the actuality of its members and organs. In the New Testament, therefore, we find no relation of polarity or tension, or of mutual dependence, between the one Church and the many gifts, persons, and the like; we find only a one-sided relation of dependence and derivation in which the many are subordinate to the one. The many have no need of an independence which indeed they do not possess, and could only achieve by lapsing away from the unity. From 1 Corinthians we know how decisively St. Paul set himself to extirpate the germs of such a development, and in that case he was only dealing with separate parties; he was not even remotely thinking of separate churches. Thus it is inevitable that any persons who think they possess, or are the Church, must look away from the array of the many churches in a quest for the *one* Church.

But what is meant by the quest for the one Church? It cannot be concerned with the magical fascination of numerical unity or uniqueness, nor with the ethical and social ideals of uniformity, mental harmony, and agreement. It must rather be concerned with the imperative content of the acknowledgment that there is one Lord, one faith, one baptism, one God above all, for all, and in all (Eph. 4:5-6). Unity in itself will not suffice: nor will any or all of the ideas and ideals which we may link with that concept. Unity in itself, even church unity in itself, is, as surely as the independent multiplicities are, merely fallen and unreconciled human nature. The quest for the unity of the Church must not be a quest for church unity in itself; for as such it is idle and empty. On the road to such a "church unity in itself" we shall find that both the powers of sin and the powers of grace are against us, and against us irresistibly.

The quest for the unity of the Church must in fact be identical with the quest for Jesus Christ as the concrete Head and Lord of the Church. The blessing of unity cannot be separated from Him who blesses, for in Him it has its source and reality, through His Word and Spirit it is revealed to us, and only in faith in Him can it become a reality among us. I repeat: Jesus Christ as the one Mediator between God and man is the oneness of the Church, is that unity within which there may be a multiplicity of communities, of gifts, of persons within one Church, while through it a multiplicity of churches are excluded. When we confess and assert that it belongs to the Church's commission to be one Church, we must not have in mind the idea of unity, whatever its goodness and moral beauty may be — we must have Him in our mind; for in Him and in Him only do those multiplicities within the Church possess their life, their scope, their dignity, rightfulness, and promise, when they seek and possess these things in that relation of dependence, derivation, subordination of which I have spoken; just as

14

man's nature, taken up by Him, united with Him and reconciled, can only find its salvation in a similar dependentness of being, scope, and significance. And in Him, in Him only, can those other multiplicities of the Church whether recent or of long standing, which claim an independence of their own, lose their life. "Homesickness for the *una sancta*" is genuine and legitimate only insofar as it is a disquietude at the fact that we have lost and forgotten Christ, and with Him have lost the unity of the Church.

Thus we must be on our guard, all along the line, lest the motives which stir us today lead us to a quest which looks past Him. Indeed, however rightful and urgent those motives are, we could well leave them out of our reckoning. We shall do well to realize that in themselves they are well-meaning but merely human desires, and that we can have no final certainty that they are

rightful, no unanswerable claim for their fulfillment. Unless we regard them with a measure of
holy indifference we are ill-placed for a quest after the unity of the Church. But we cannot leave
out of our reckoning the claim urged by Jesus
Christ upon us. If we listen to the voice of the
Good Shepherd, then the question of the unity of
the Church will most surely become for us a
burning question. Then, it may be, His voice will
endorse those motives of which we have spoken,
with weight, necessity, and imperative force; it
will then be right and requisite that they should
kindle us to a flame, and any indifference to them
will be far from holy. From that Voice which
alone can question us in tones which make "our
hearts burn within us" must we expect and await
the ultimate answer. ◇

The Multiplicity
of the Churches

We have no right to explain the multiplicity of the churches as a necessary mark of the visible and empirical as contrasted with the ideal, invisible, and essential Church; no right, because this entire distinction is foreign to the New Testament, and because, according to the New Testament, even in this respect the Church of Jesus Christ is but one; invisible in respect of the grace of the Word of God and of the Holy Spirit, whereby the Church and its members as such are grounded, up-borne, guided, and preserved, but visible by tokens in the multitude of its confessed adherents, visible as a congregation with its office-bearers, visible as a ministry of Word and Sacrament. It is indeed an act of *faith* that where these things are found, there the Church is; but on the other hand it is only in virtue of the tokens which thus manifest it as existent and active that we can make that act of faith.

There is no way of escape from the visible to the invisible Church. Our questioning, therefore, as to the unity of the Church cannot be silenced by pointing away to the invisible or essential Church. If there is a problem here which asks for solution — and indeed there is — it is one which concerns the invisible as directly as it concerns the visible Church; if we hearken to Christ, we shall be sure of that, and only if we prefer to platonize shall we deny it.

But, further, we have no right to explain the multiplicity of the churches as an unfolding of the wealth of that grace which is given to mankind in Jesus Christ, divinely purposed and therefore normal. How can we know that the case stands thus? What is our standing ground if we take the familiar line of ascribing to the Roman, the Greek, the Lutheran, the Reformed, the Anglican, and other churches their special attributes

and functions within an imagined organic total-
ity? However well this may sound, it is not theology, it is mere sociology or philosophy of history; it means that in order to evade the question
of church unity we are spinning the thread of our
own notions instead of facing the question with
which Christ confronts us, and listening for His
own answer. But if we did face it, we should be
quite sure that it is utterly and forever impossible
to take the Virgin of Einsiedeln and Luther's
Wittenberg or Calvin's Geneva, the Roman Mass
and the Evangelical Communion, the Orthodox
inconostasis and the evangelical pulpit, the poly-
theism of the "Deutsche Christen" (including
those who in fact though not in name belong to
them) and the evangelical interpretation of the
first commandment, as branches of the one and
the self-same tree, comparing and estimating
them as belonging to one category. At these

points as at others the multiplicity of the churches is manifest, and — if we listen to Christ — it demands from us a definite decision and choice, this way or that. If we listen to Christ, we cannot believe in one of the alternatives and hold the other also to be Christian; our life is lived within the differences which divide the churches, and not in a region which transcends them. Such a region has for its inhabitants only those who, in contemplation of God and their own selves, come at the last to prefer their own voices to any other.

In fact, we have no right to explain the multiplicity of the churches at all. We have to deal with it as we deal with sin, our own and others', to recognize it as a fact, to understand it as the impossible thing which has intruded itself, as guilt which we must take upon ourselves, without the power to liberate ourselves from it. We must not allow ourselves to acquiesce in its reality; rather we must pray that it be forgiven and removed, and be ready to do whatever God's will and command may enjoin in respect of it. A great part, the decisive part perhaps, of all that men can do for the unity of the Church would be already done, if on all sides we were able and willing to handle the multiplicity of the churches in this way: no longer as a speculative problem or a matter of the philosophy of history, but, to put it in the simplest terms, with a sober mind, as men profoundly shocked but yet believing, and therefore hopeful, and, by reason of hope, ready to obey.

Or is there perhaps some other possible way than that of dealing with the multiplicity of the churches as we deal with sin, our own and others'? If Christ is indeed, as we saw, the unity of the Church, then the only multiplicity which can be normal is that *within* the Church, namely that of

23

the local communities, of the gifts of the Spirit, of the believers of each sex, language, and race, and there can be no multiplicity of churches. It is then unthinkable that to those multiplicities which are rooted in unity we should have to add that which tears it in pieces; unthinkable that great entire groups of communities should stand over against each other in such a way that their doctrines and confessions of faith are mutually contradictory; that what is called revelation in one place should be called error elsewhere, that what is here revered as dogma should there be regarded as heresy; that the ordinances of one group should be stigmatized by another as alien, unacceptable, or even intolerable: that the adherents of the one should be at one with those of another in every conceivable point except that they are unable to pray together, to preach and hear God's word together, and to join together in Holy Communion.

The Multiplicity of the Churches

It is unthinkable that whichever way one looks and listens, one should hear people saying, in quiet or vehement tones, with kindly understatement or undisguised sternness, "You have a different Spirit from ours." Yet that is just what actually results from the multiplicity of the churches; to wash our hands of it, or to prescribe doses of love, patience, and tolerance as a cure, is futile. Such prescriptions may serve our turn almost anywhere else, but it is hopeless to mediate between the churches by such methods — unless the churches are dead already. If they are alive, and if we are listening for Christ's voice, then it is not a matter of opinion but of faith that over against the doctrine, order, and life of other churches we should utter a more or less emphatic No at certain decision points, that we should draw the line and thus be compelled to endorse the multiplicity of the churches. As I said before, the truth of God in Jesus Christ compels us again and again to decision and choice; thus men's minds go diverse ways, not perversely (if all is clean and above board), not without pain, yet unaffectedly, unmoved by the possible reproach of narrow-mindedness and want of heart, lending no ear to those who cry "peace, peace" when there is no peace. Men's minds, at such points, must needs go different ways: the churches must needs separate or abide by an existing separation. This is our trouble, this "needs must" which comes from Christ, and makes hard fact of a state of things which, if Christ is our starting-point, our minds admit to be unthinkable.

I know that we must bear it in mind that the Church is the existential form of the Kingdom of Christ in the interim between the Ascension and His second coming, that is, in an epoch in which He is no longer present with us in that mode wherein He was present to His disciples and apostles in the great forty days, nor is He yet so present as He will be in the manifested, and so far perfected glory of His Kingdom. But it is just the incompleteness, the burden and trouble of this epoch which is manifested in the multiplicity of the churches, as it is also manifest in the original and actual sin even of believers, even of the members of Christ's body. All the more must we treat this incompleteness seriously, all the more must we think of it and deal with it as linked together with sin, because our vision looks past it in hope, though in a hope as yet unfulfilled.

I know too that we should also bear it in mind, that over against the terrible multiplicity of the churches, signs of oneness are not wholly absent. Let us always be ready to admit with gratitude that there are points of agreement between all churches, agreements often between churches which are most distant from each other and in serious conflict; they shine out, at moments, in the gloom, with surpassing clearness. However dreadfully the separations which lie behind them may reassert themselves, these visions should not be forgotten or underestimated; we need only remember that these agreements — they are signs and nothing more — can neither remove our trouble, our inevitable separateness in faith, hope, and love, nor make manifest the unity of the Church.

Let us lastly bear in mind a truth which even in the strongest stress of ecclesiastical controversy has hardly ever been ignored or denied, that there are real Christians, God's elect, in all the churches, who, dispersed though they may be, do yet give a visible expression to the unity of the Church. But, admitting this, what are we to say of the rest and what of the churches as such? Are

28

we, like the hyper-puritans of all ages, to think of
the rest as lost? And if we refuse to call them lost,
what are we to make of the fact that those real
Christians, as such, plainly count for nothing in
face of the separateness of the churches?

Faced by this trouble, it will be well for us to
stand and confront it as an enigma which no the-
ory will help us to solve. If we could deduce the
multiplicity of the churches as logically emerging
from the unity; if we could find the truth of the
ecclesia sancta catholica, the *communio sanctorum* unfolding its implications in a *sic* and a *non,* and in a
synthesis transcending them both, in such a way
that the parallel and contradictory phenomena of
Rome and Byzantium, Wittenberg and Geneva,
episcopacy and presbyterianism, Reformation
Protestantism and Protestant modernism, with
many more antitheses, could be regarded as the
fruits of a logical necessity, past and present, then

there would be no real trouble to confront us. But there is. There is a trouble which we have to face in action, in action only; and the first and last thing in our response as we face it must be prayer for forgiveness and sanctification offered up to the Lord of the Church. The multiplicity of the churches is simply our helplessness in His sight. We cannot listen for His voice, without an act of decision, choice, confession: yet we cannot decide and confess our faith without falling into separation and so coming into contradiction against Him. Who are we, and what is His Church, if that is our standing towards Him? We had best attempt to give no other answer than this, that we are those, that the Church is the congregation of those, who know that they are helpless, but that they are helpless in the presence of One who as their Savior and their Lord is greater than they. ◈

✦ III ✦

The Union
of the Churches — A Task

If Jesus Christ is the unity of the Church, and if the multiplicity of the churches is our trouble, then there can be no evading the fact that the union of the churches into a Church is a task imposed by the Lord of the Church and therefore a mandate. It is not implied that we can and shall fulfill this command: nor, certainly, is it implied that all or any of the things which have been and are being attempted towards church union are even partially or approximately such a fulfillment. Rather must we constantly remember that the fulfillment of the command is wholly and entirely the work of Him who lays it on us, that in Him the Church is once for all, and in spite of every multiplicity of the churches, made one, and does not await any desires, capacities, or labors of ours for its unification. And yet our faith in Jesus Christ brings with it this implication, that the command is indubitably laid upon us, and that we have a share, not by virtue of any Christian activity of ours, but in faith in Jesus Christ, in its fulfillment. We cannot accept the assurance of our justification, on the ground of the righteousness which is perfected in Jesus Christ alone, without hearing His command, and learning that even as we accept it we are claimed through Him, claimed therefore for the unity of the Church; since we belong no longer to ourselves but to Him, our action, remote though it may be, in itself, from His, is directed inevitably towards the uniting of the Church.

But what is the union of the churches? Was it a deliberate acceptance and initiation of the task, when from the 18th century onwards, the churches began to adopt the idea of mutual civility and tolerance? There is no need to ignore the advantageous results of that development; yet the serious criticism to which this mode of union is open cannot be ignored. The concept of toleration originates in political and philosophical principles which are not only alien but even opposed to the Gospel. Their triumph within the various churches was a symptom of inward weakness and not of strength. Among its results is one which ought not to be overlooked, namely that the churches have in increasing measure lost their character and their significance in the life of the peoples; and just in proportion as the churches awoke to fresh self-consciousness as holders of a confession, so did it become manifest that tolerance, so far from removing the old separations, had not affected them in the least.

Much the same thing has to be said of those federations or alliances of which every country has for some time afforded examples, alliances between separated churches as such or between religious societies here and there which foster similar activities, e.g., those of home or foreign missions. Is the focus in which men have thus made contact or even achieved coalitions with each other, the essential point? Clearly it is not; for otherwise they would have gone on to establish quite other coalitions and contacts. But if it is not the essential, if, as may well be, it is only something which the Church has in common with human societies and undertakings in general, if it is only the better sort of humanitarian motive and effort that leads to such contacts and agreements, then what can they really effect toward the uniting of the Church? A mere federation, in itself, has nothing at all to do with real church union. We may find a clear indication of this in the fact that even so strong and energetic a coalition as that which in recent years has brought German Lutherans and Reformed together in the Confessional Synods has not yet resulted in united Communion services, but rather (so far, at least, as the Lutherans are concerned) in a fresh, if not entirely sincere, awaking of denominational self-consciousness.

Must we speak in similar terms of what is called the ecumenical movement? The more cautious and modest its aims, the less it indulges in shouting "hallelujah" — as has been all too prematurely done, alike in the age of tolerance and in that of federation — the more chance there will be of avoiding this danger. That those who differ in belief should come to know each other in the matters which are essential to each, should give a fair hearing to what is essential in other churches, should confer with persons consciously and definitely representing such churches, in quest for that unity which each of them so variously and with such differing claims intends to represent; all this even when attempted only on the scale of personal intercourse, was to the good, and it would be well that so promising a method should be utilized on a larger scale. But this would lead to one of two results; we should either be left with a few statements of religious and denominational import, precise, interesting, and yet irresponsible, or we should find that the various churches, having learned to understand each other more thoroughly, were more conscious than ever of their own *differentiae* and their inevitable separateness. The union of the churches is too great a matter to be the result of a movement, however cautious and far-sighted. Formal resolutions and declarations made by the various organs of the ecumenical movement could only serve as the anticipation of such a result; and as such they cannot possess that validity which alone could entitle them to be received and taken by the various churches, not merely as courageous expressions of humanitarianisms such as a Commission of the League of Nations might put out, but as coming from the authoritative voice of the one Church.

From this point of view I am not distressed by the well-known and widely regretted attitude of the Roman See towards union movements of the past and present. It was and is needful that some-one somewhere should make a stand against the excessive claims of all church movements, and assert that the union of the churches is a thing which cannot be manufactured, but must be found and confessed, in subordination to that already accomplished oneness of the Church which is in Jesus Christ. It is in this sense that I understand the papal refusal to take a hand in the efforts which have been hitherto made towards union. And in this sense I would say that in those circles which are rightly preoccupied with the thought of union it is impossible to be too cautious about "open" Communion services and the like. Much that is beautiful in itself is a very long way from being true, far therefore from being enjoined upon us or even permissible.

Let us not deceive ourselves. The union of the churches into the oneness of the Church would mean more than mutual tolerance, respect, and cooperation; more than readiness to hear and to understand each other; more than an emotional sense of oneness in the possession of some ineffable common link; more than that we, being one in faith, hope, and charity, could worship together in one accord. Above all it would mean, as the decisive test of unity, that we should join in making confession of our faith and thus should unitedly proclaim it to the world, and so fulfill that commandment of Jesus on which the Church is based. The message and witness, given by the Church's teaching, order, and life, must utter one voice, however manifold in the diversity of languages, gifts, places, and persons. A union of the churches in the sense of that task which is so seriously laid upon the Church would mean a union of the confessions into one unanimous confession. If we remain on the level where confessions are divided, we remain where the multiplicity of the churches is inevitable.

Let us clear our minds. What are the essential conditions in which it would be possible to share in such a genuine effort of union towards a living Church, call it what you will?

(1) Suppose a church to be taking the step of relinquishing its own particular confession for one which it will share in union with others. Such a step ought in no circumstances to be an act of confessional weakness, an assertion of indifference to its faith and apprehension. Rather, the

Church should feel itself called, instructed, and summoned, in its special place and responsibility, to act with seriousness in the power of an enhanced, not of a diminished faith. So and not otherwise should it be led past its own particularity towards oneness.

(2) No secular motive, such as the desire for national or international union, should be allowed to prompt a church to surrender its individuality. Modestly though the claim should be made, a genuine church separation will always possess a preponderant rightness over against any non-churchly motives for union, and only through its faith can and must a living church know itself to be called to abandon its separateness.

(3) Such a surrender must not imply the abandonment, in one iota, of anything which a church believes it necessary to assert in a certain way and

not otherwise. The step away from a particular to a common confession must have no taint of compromise, or of an assent to forms and formulae of union which would camouflage division without transcending it. A church taking such a step must be known to act with perfect truthfulness and loyalty.

(4) In the surrender of separation only one thing must be abandoned, namely a failure in obedience to Christ, hitherto unrealized, in which a church, in common, it may be, with a neighbor church, or with all the severed churches, has had a share of guilt in that trouble which is the multiplicity of the churches. Its share has possibly lain in the fact that the normal and necessary multiplicity of communities, gifts, and persons within the Church has by the agency of the evil one been perverted; possibly in this, that undue place and import has been attributed to what is racial, to ele-

ments of human mentality and ethic, or of historical persistence. This would be the disobedience which the church would have to consider, as it listened afresh to the voice of Christ.

It is beyond controversy that only through the satisfaction of these conditions could a living church be led to unite with other churches. But the conditions are plainly such as to make the union of the churches a task which is lofty and arduous beyond measure: a task of super-human magnitude, we may say, as we reflect on the facts of multiplicity, or as each of us thinks of his own church, a living church as one may hope, and therefore one which would approach these conditions without laxity. What voice or summons will be mighty enough to utter God's word in such tones to a church like the Roman, the Lutheran, or the Reformed, to these three together and all the others with them, that in conformity with these conditions they could respond with *one* confession and so return to the unity of the Church? Yet if such a voice is not uttered and heard, they neither can nor may rightly unite. A union which presupposed less than this would be no act of obedience but a juggling with the facts.

If these things are so, then we do not evade the question concerning the task of church union; we answer it in the only possible way, if we revert to the principle that in Christ alone this task is fulfilled, that His voice and summons alone can bring that union into being. All that we do in this matter will be good or evil in proportion as it makes it possible for us and for others to listen to that summons and that voice. ◈

✢   **IV**   ✢

The Church
in the Churches

The task of church union is essentially one with that concrete practical task which all church activity must presuppose, the task of listening to Christ: they move or halt together. But it follows from this that the question of the quest for the Church must be definitely raised and find an answer within the churches, in their present multiplicity and separation. We cannot hear Christ otherwise than according to the particular leading and responsibility of the churches, each of us, that is, giving ear to the church to which we owe allegiance as members, within which we were baptized and brought to belief. Whether we like it or not, whether we share or not in a common disobedience and sin, whether our yearning for the *una sancta* is deep or shallow, we are all in separation; our churchly existence, so far as we have one at all, is a separated one; only in our own church can we listen to Christ, not in any other, and still less on any neutral ground above or outside the severed churches. This holds good, I believe — insofar as the distinction is permissible — for the personal and individual faith and life of each of us one by one; certainly it holds good for that "hearing of Christ" which we are now discussing, namely for a "hearing" which is the presupposition of all church activity and therefore of work for the union of the churches. If a man says that he can hear Christ's voice as well in this or that church as in his own, he had better ask himself whether he has not come to substitute for the obedient mind and will which listens to Christ (in his own and other churches) one or other of the many available historical or aesthetic interests. As for a neutral ground outside or above the churches, in such a sphere committees and conferences may be held, or Christian men and women, yet more irresponsible and unauthoritative, may follow their own ideas and schemes. But such inter- and supra-denominational movements as thus come into being are either ineffective because they do not seriously tackle the problems of the Church, of doctrine, of order and life, or they have an effect because they do take them seriously, and lo and behold, they are engaged in forming a church; a new church or church-like society comes into being, and neutrality is abandoned, and the old question regarding unity is met with another which concerns the movement which is trying to give unity a visible shape. Church work, and union work as a part of it, must be done within the churches, in its proper Christian home, or it will not be done at all. If we would listen to Christ, as to Him who Himself is the Church's unity and in whom its union is already accomplished, then from the outset we must with humble but complete sincerity endorse the confession of our own

51

church. Admittedly, what we thus endorse is a painful thing; it lacks finality, and the hope of transcending it will rightly be present to our minds; it involves the confession of our own and our fathers' sin — shall we say a hidden sin, or one which has long parted with concealment? And yet only thus can we endorse the call of Christ, for it is only thus that (however human errors and perplexities may obscure it) the call reaches us. So long as it is true that Christ calls us so, we can only confess Him by endorsing the confession of our own church. But if He has called us otherwise, then there is another church, whose confession we ought to endorse instead of our own. We shall do very poor service to the cause of union if we think meanly of the sphere and church assigned to us, and attempt to stage the unity of the Church or play the part of the Christ ourselves.

Coming now to the problem of *life* then, the

question which each church should put to itself is this: Do we, as a church, in our relation and attitude to the realities and problems of the church's environment in the world, really listen to Christ in the terms of our own tradition and confession?

Do we allow Christ (not, of course, any artificial Christ, but the Christ of those scriptures which our own and all other churches accept) to determine our relation to the state — a part of our environment which is present to all our minds just now — as our confession requires and our standards have declared? Or, in this connection as in others, do we allow ourselves to follow a line of tactics or strategy in which we do in fact listen for other voices, respectable perhaps, but alien from Christ? It comes to this: If two or three churches, be they never so different and divided, were to put just this question penitently to themselves, then *ipso facto* in those *churches* the *Church* would be a present reality and visible. In Germany, Lutheran and Reformed came wonderfully close to each other in recent years, just in proportion as they (starting from the Lutheran and Reformed confessions respectively) found themselves faced with the practical decision which Christ laid upon them. Perhaps other churches only require a little more of that alertness which tribulation calls forth, that awareness of the straight dealing which a church when challenged must exhibit, in order to experience something of the Church and its oneness, without any union or in anticipation of any efforts in that direction.

Again, in respect of *order,* every church should ask itself, quite simply, this question: Are we really listening to Christ, as we in the spirit of our church and in accord with its direction deal thus with the congregations, their ministries, and their worship? Are we serious in saying that our papal, episcopal, presbyterian system, or (if we are Quakers) our lack of system is the true representation of the Lordship of Christ in His Church? Do we respect His Lordship as we say that we do, when we think it vital to make the sacrament or the liturgy or the sermon the focus of our worship? Or, when we follow our conscience or the best of our knowledge and adopt this or that line as the right order, is it rather a naive and secular turn of mind that influences us, whether it be monarchical, democratic, or individualist? Is it Christ who dominates us, or just some magical, aesthetic, or rationalistic bent? I assert that if only each church will take itself seriously, "itself, and Christ within it," then even if there be no talk of union movements in it, even if there be no change at all in its order and its way of worship, the one Church would be in that single church a present reality and visible. So long as it passes no judgment on itself and is zealous for its own ordinances as such, it can only represent the multiplicity of the churches. But within the multiplicity it can represent the unity of the Church, if in its ordinances it is zealous for Christ.

Each several church should ask itself the same question with regard to the central problem of doctrine. It may sound like perilous relativism, yet of this problem also I will say the same thing — let the Roman church work out its doctrine of nature and grace, with the Tridentine teaching on justification, to their logical conclusions; let the Lutheran and Calvinistic bodies do the same with their specific eucharistic doctrine, and neo-Protestantism with its doctrine of man's natural goodness; but let them do this not merely in a syllogistic spirit, nor as working with logical fervor on the basis of presuppositions which stop short of being ultimate, but as listening to Christ, to

Christ of the scriptures. The confessions will then come into the open, over against each other, in sharp and surprising contrast; and that is precisely what makes many people regard them, and regard serious theology, with disquietude and reluctance, in the interest of peace. Yet, strange as it may seem, it is still true, that those who fail to understand other churches than their own are not the people who care intensely about theology, but the theological dilettantes, eclectics, and historians of all sorts; while those very men who have found themselves forced to confront a clear thoroughgoing logical *sic et non* find themselves allied to each other in spite of all contradictions, by an underlying fellowship and understanding, even in the cause which they handle so differently and approach from such painfully different angles. But that cause, it may be, is nothing else than Jesus Christ and the unity of the Church. For my part I am convinced that true unity was more of a present and visible reality in the Marburg discussions of 1529 — which it is fashionable to decry — or in the polemics of later Lutheran and Reformed orthodoxy — for which no one has a good word — than in certain doings of our own day, in which there was so much profession of charity that no one had courage enough left to enquire with serious honesty about the truth, or to allow thesis and antithesis well thought out to meet each other face to face. But to enquire into the truth of Christ is always hopeful, always a work of charity; it is always and in all circumstances a service to the union of the churches, even when its first result is that no one moves an inch from his thesis, and so the fact of division is at first accentuated.

The third postulate is this — and if it is scripturally true that the Church's decisive and ultimate function is that of teaching and preaching, I may call it the fundamental postulate and presupposition of church union: it is vital that once more in every church, in its own special atmosphere and thus with an ear attentive to Christ, real sober strict genuine theology should become active. Theological work, concrete and unpretentious, may well be the business which men can most readily set about within the churches for the sake of the Church. Here I make an abrupt end; thus leaving it clear that even in this sphere the really decisive work cannot be an achievement of human power. ◈